Aaron Rodgers

By Jeff Savage

AMAZING
ATHLETES

⌐ Lerner Publications Company • Minneapolis

Lerner Publications Company
A division of Lerner Publishing Group, Inc.
241 First Avenue North
Minneapolis, MN 55401 U.S.A.

Website address: www.lernerbooks.com

Library of Congress Cataloging-in-Publication Data

Savage, Jeff, 1961–
    Aaron Rodgers / by Jeff Savage.
        p.   cm. — (Amazing athletes)
    Includes index.
    ISBN 978–0–7613–8223–2 (lib. bdg. : alk. paper)
    1. Rodgers, Aaron, 1983– 2. Football players—United States—Biography—Juvenile literature.
    3. Quarterbacks (Football)—United States—Biography—Juvenile literature. I. Title.
    GV939.R6235S28 2012
    796.332092—dc22
        [B]   2011006453

Manufactured in the United States of America
1 – BP – 7/15/11

TABLE OF CONTENTS

Super Performance   4

Football Dreams   9

Finding His Way   13

Getting Better   19

Sweet Journey   24

Selected Career Highlights   29
Glossary   30
Further Reading & Websites   31
Index   32

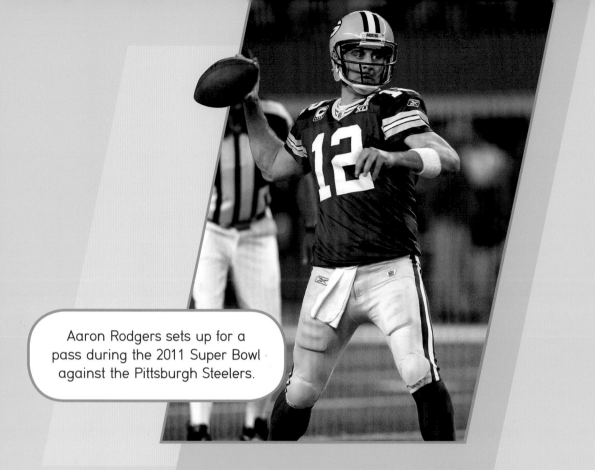

Aaron Rodgers sets up for a pass during the 2011 Super Bowl against the Pittsburgh Steelers.

SUPER PERFORMANCE

Aaron Rodgers threw a perfect **spiral**. Packers **receiver** Jordy Nelson was running deep down the right side of the field. The football landed directly in Nelson's arms. But with 111 million people watching, Nelson dropped it.

Aaron and his Green Bay Packers teammates were playing against the Pittsburgh Steelers in Super Bowl XLV on February 6, 2011. The Steelers had the top defense in football. The Packers could hardly afford to drop easy passes. Unfortunately, they dropped five perfect throws from Aaron in the game. But Aaron wasn't about to let mistakes rattle him in the biggest game of his life.

Jordy Nelson of the Packers misses a catch on a pass from Aaron during the Super Bowl.

Nelson carries the ball for a **touchdown** on a throw from Aaron.

When the Packers got the ball again, Aaron completed four passes to move the ball down the field. In the **huddle**, he called for a short pass play. But he changed the play at the **line of scrimmage**. Aaron threw another deep pass to Nelson. This time, Nelson caught it for a 29-yard touchdown! Aaron threw his arms in the air. With the extra point, the Packers led 7–0.

Twenty-four seconds later, Nick Collins **intercepted** Steelers quarterback Ben Roethlisberger's pass. He weaved his way 37 yards into the **end zone**. That put the Packers ahead, 14–0.

The Steelers answered with a **field goal**. Then Donald Driver, one of Aaron's favorite receivers, limped off the field with an ankle injury. Aaron stayed calm. He fired down the middle to Greg Jennings. Touchdown!

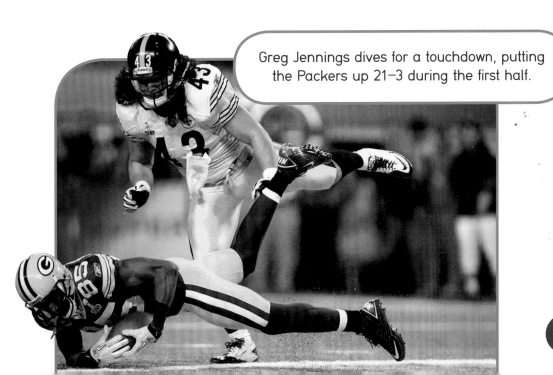

Greg Jennings dives for a touchdown, putting the Packers up 21–3 during the first half.

Pittsburgh fought back, cutting the lead to 21–17. Aaron responded with another drive. At the 8-yard line, he looked left. Then he turned right. Aaron zipped a pass to Jennings for another touchdown.

The Packers won the Super Bowl, 31–25. Aaron was named Most Valuable Player (MVP). "This is what I dreamed about as a kid," he said. "This is incredible."

Aaron and teammate Clay Matthews *(left)* celebrate the Packers' Super Bowl victory.

This photo shows Aaron's hometown of Chico, California, at night.

FOOTBALL DREAMS

Aaron Charles Rodgers was born December 2, 1983, to Ed and Darla Rodgers. Aaron grew up in Chico, California, with his parents and his brothers, Luke and Jordan.

Aaron loved football from the start. San Francisco 49ers quarterback Joe Montana was his hero. In kindergarten, Aaron played football at recess. He was always quarterback.

Aaron excelled at other sports too. By second grade, he could dribble a basketball with either hand and throw passes without looking. As a Little League baseball pitcher, he fired balls past batters.

Aaron often played with his older brother Luke. Dad threw football passes while the two boys covered each other. But Luke controlled basketball games. "I wanted to beat him so bad," Aaron said. "If he beat me, I'd make him stay out there and play game after game."

In high school, Aaron traveled to Mexico twice with other area youths to help build houses for poor families.

As a freshman at Pleasant Valley High School in Chico in 1998, Aaron was just five feet eight and weighed 135 pounds. But he wore size 14 shoes. Some friends called him Feet.

Aaron suffered a serious knee injury in his sophomore football season. A doctor told him to take a year off from sports. Instead, Aaron wore a brace and strengthened his knee with exercises. He was back on the field as a junior. Aaron passed for over 2,000 yards that season. He focused on football more than ever. He skipped parties to get a good night's sleep.

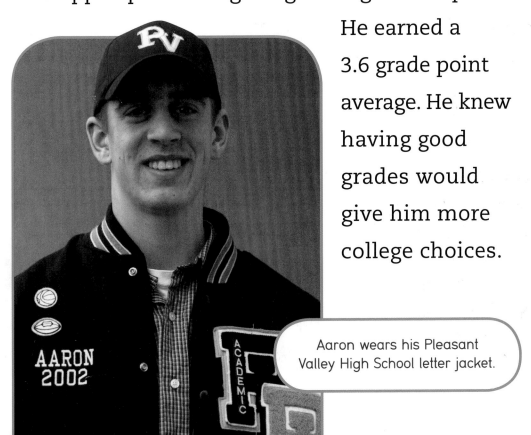

He earned a 3.6 grade point average. He knew having good grades would give him more college choices.

Aaron wears his Pleasant Valley High School letter jacket.

As a senior in 2001, Aaron passed for 2,303 yards to break the school record. He threw six touchdowns in one game to set another record. He waited for **college recruiters** to offer him **scholarships**. But no one called or visited.

A young Aaron looks for a target in a game against the Red Bluff Spartans. Red Bluff is northwest of Chico.

Aaron also pitched for his high school baseball team. Here he winds up for a pitch in a game against Paradise High School, from Paradise, California, just east of Chico.

FINDING HIS WAY

Aaron was heartbroken by the lack of interest from colleges. Recruiters just didn't visit Chico. And coaches may have thought Aaron wasn't big enough. He had grown to be six feet one and 185 pounds, still small for a college quarterback. He thought about a future in baseball. He could pitch a ball at 90 miles per hour.

Playing for Butte Community College in 2002, Aaron outruns an opponent.

Craig Rigsbee was the football coach at nearby Butte Community College. Rigsbee convinced Aaron to play **junior college** football at Butte. In 2002, Aaron passed for 2,408 yards and 28 touchdowns with just four interceptions. "He commanded our team," said Coach Rigsbee. "If I accidentally sent in the wrong play, he'd wave to me and say, 'Don't worry. I know what you meant.'"

Aaron led Butte to a 10–1 record and No. 2 national ranking. "That's where I got my confidence," said Aaron. "And I've never lost it."

One day at practice, Aaron saw University of California–Berkeley (Cal) coach Jeff Tedford on the side of the field. Coach Tedford was at Butte to recruit one of Aaron's teammates. Tedford was amazed watching Aaron direct the plays.

Aaron talks with Cal coach Jeff Tedford.

He told Rigsbee, "That's the best junior college quarterback I've ever seen." Tedford called Aaron on the drive home and offered him a scholarship to Cal. Aaron accepted.

Aaron became Cal's starting quarterback midway through the 2003 season. He led the Golden Bears to victory over the University of Illinois. The following week, he led a shocking 34–31 upset of No. 3-ranked University of Southern California (USC) in triple overtime! Aaron helped the Golden Bears win eight games, including the Insight Bowl. He threw just five interceptions all season, a school record.

Aaron makes a pass against the USC Trojans.

The Golden Bears were highly ranked in the 2004 **polls**. "Nobody's expectations can exceed what I want out of myself," said Aaron. He wanted to play like Joe Montana. Aaron even wore a Joe Montana shirt under his Cal jersey.

Aaron led the Golden Bears to their best season in 50 years. Their only loss was a close game at No. 1-ranked USC. In the game, Aaron completed 23 straight passes. No college quarterback had ever completed more passes in a row.

Aaron learned an important lesson in college about staying positive. In a loss to Oregon State, he sat alone on the bench. He didn't talk to his teammates. Afterward, coach Tedford talked to Aaron about his pouting. "When we're going through tough times," he explained, "people are looking to you to provide leadership." Aaron changed that day.

Aaron led Cal to a 41–6 blowout in what fans call the Big Game, the annual game against rival Stanford University. Golden Bears fans swarmed the field afterward and lifted him in the air. They chanted "One more year, one more year!" They hoped Aaron would stay at Cal for his senior season. But Aaron was ready for the NFL.

Carrying their star quarterback, Aaron, Golden Bears fans celebrate a big win over the Stanford Cardinal.

Aaron holds up the jersey for his new team— the Green Bay Packers.

GETTING BETTER

Most people agreed there were two top quarterbacks in the 2005 NFL **Draft**. One was University of Utah's Alex Smith. The other was Aaron. The San Francisco 49ers owned the first pick in the draft. They chose Smith. Other teams passed on Aaron. Finally, with the twenty-fourth pick, the Green Bay Packers selected him.

Brett Favre was the quarterback of the Packers. Fans were crazy about him. But the Packers needed a promising young backup who could be their next star. They signed Aaron to a five-year **contract** for $7.7 million. It was a lot of money to pay a player to sit on the bench. For two seasons, Aaron watched Favre play. Aaron learned what he could.

Green Bay's star quarterback Brett Favre *(left)* sits beside Aaron on the sidelines during a game against the New Orleans Saints in 2005.

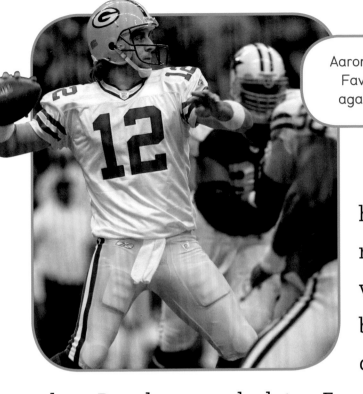

Aaron took over for an injured Favre during a 2007 game against the Dallas Cowboys.

In 2007, Favre hinted he might retire. Aaron would get to be starting quarterback at last. But three weeks later, Favre decided to keep playing. Aaron went back to the bench. He did not show any frustration.

In a game against the Dallas Cowboys, Favre got hurt. Aaron took over and carved up the Cowboys' defense. He completed 18 passes for 201 yards. Aaron proved he could lead the team. But he went back to the bench for the rest of the season.

During training camp in 2008, many Packers fans held signs and wore T-shirts asking the team to bring back Favre.

In March 2008, Favre officially retired. But he changed his mind again in July. The Packers hinted that it was time to move on. Fans wanted Favre. Some fans booed Aaron at practice.

Aaron was caught in the middle. He kept quiet. In early August, the team announced that Aaron would be Green Bay's starter. Favre was traded to the New York Jets.

Many fans were angry. But Aaron's teammates admired him. He kept his cool through it all.

Aaron played well from the start. On October 31, the Packers signed him to a contract **extension** for six years and $65 million. "I told them I would repay them for their trust," Aaron said. The Packers finished with a 6–10 record. But Aaron was brilliant. He passed for 28 touchdowns and over 4,000 yards.

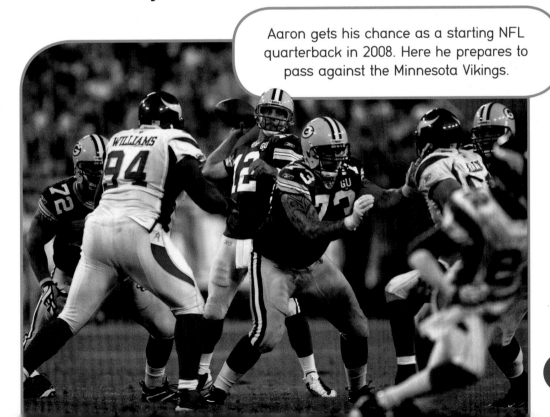

Aaron gets his chance as a starting NFL quarterback in 2008. Here he prepares to pass against the Minnesota Vikings.

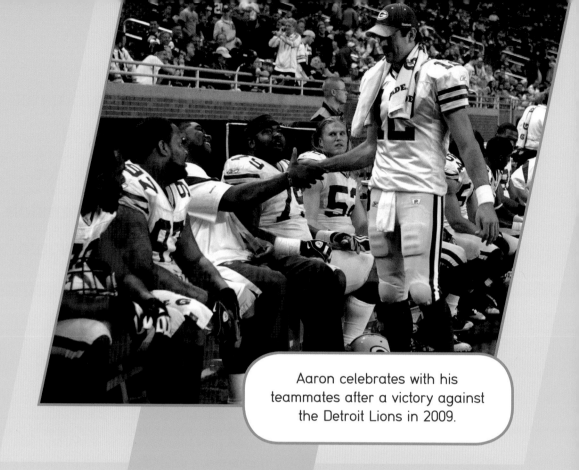

Aaron celebrates with his teammates after a victory against the Detroit Lions in 2009.

SWEET JOURNEY

The Packers were Aaron's team now. In 2009, he led the Packers to an 11–5 record and the **playoffs**. Green Bay lost to Arizona in overtime in the **wild-card game**, 51–45. But Aaron threw for 423 yards in the game, a Packers playoff record.

The Packers had high hopes for 2010. But in the first game, **running back** Ryan Grant was lost for the season with an injury. **Tight end** Jermichael Finley was lost a few games later. Then Aaron suffered two **concussions** in losses to the Washington Redskins and the Detroit Lions. The Packers lost again without Aaron the week after the Lion's game. They had to win their last two games to sneak into the playoffs. They did.

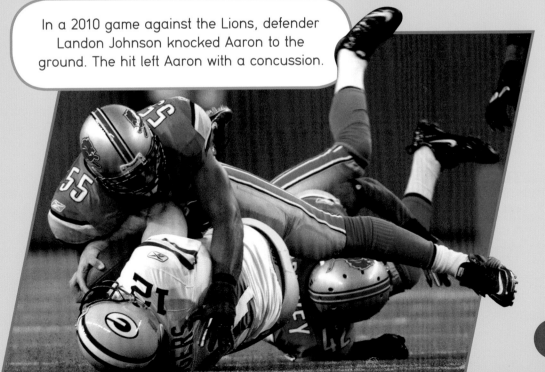

In a 2010 game against the Lions, defender Landon Johnson knocked Aaron to the ground. The hit left Aaron with a concussion.

Green Bay had to play on the road in the playoffs. Aaron didn't mind. He threw three touchdown passes to beat the Eagles in Philadelphia, 21–16. He completed 31 of 36 passes with three more touchdowns to pick apart the Falcons in Atlanta, 48–21.

Next, the Packers faced their rivals, the Bears, in icy Chicago. They were playing for the National Football Conference (NFC) Championship. Aaron led the offense on an 84-yard touchdown drive to start the game. He celebrated with his "championship belt" move. The Packers kept the lead and won, 21–14.

The Packers capped their amazing playoff run with their Super Bowl win over the Steelers. "I never doubted I could do this," Aaron said. "I just always wondered if I would get a chance."

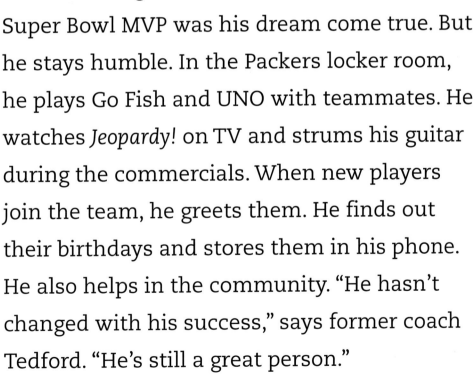

Aaron celebrates touchdowns as if he were putting on a professional wrestling championship belt.

Aaron is the NFL's all-time career leader in **passer rating**, and becoming a Super Bowl MVP was his dream come true. But he stays humble. In the Packers locker room, he plays Go Fish and UNO with teammates. He watches *Jeopardy!* on TV and strums his guitar during the commercials. When new players join the team, he greets them. He finds out their birthdays and stores them in his phone. He also helps in the community. "He hasn't changed with his success," says former coach Tedford. "He's still a great person."

After the Packers won the Super Bowl, Aaron enjoyed a moment with his family *(from left to right)*: brother Jordan, father Ed, mother Darla, and his grandparents.

Aaron welcomes challenges. "The journey is the sweetest part for me," he says. "Having to work hard for success has made it much more satisfying."

Selected Career Highlights

2010–2011 Named MVP of Super Bowl XLV
Named FedEx Air NFL Player of the Year
Led Packers to three road wins in playoffs
Completed 312 of 475 passes for 3,922
   yards and 28 touchdowns
Selected to the Pro Bowl

2009–2010 Set career highs with 350 completions,
   4,434 yards, and 30 passing touchdowns
Became the first player in NFL history with
   over 4,000 yards passing in his first two
   seasons as a starter
Selected to the Pro Bowl

2008–2009 Named Packers starting quarterback
Completed 341 of 536 passes for 4,038 yards and 28 touchdowns

2007–2008 Completed 20 of 28 passes for 218 yards and one touchdown

2006–2007 Completed 6 of 15 passes for 46 yards

2005 Drafted by the Green Bay Packers in the first round
Completed 9 of 16 passes for 65 yards

2004 Named honorable mention All-America
Named first-team All-Pac 10
Named second-team Academic All-Pac 10
Led Cal to their best season in 50 years (10-1 regular season)
Tied NCAA record for most single-game completions in a row (23)

2003 Named honorable mention All-Pac 10
Passed for career-high 394 yards against Virginia Tech in the
   Insight Bowl
Tied Cal record with five 300-yard games
Set Cal record for lowest interception rate at 1.43 percent

2002 Led Butte Community College to a 10–1 record and No. 2
   national ranking

2001 Set Pleasant Valley High School record for most passing yards in
   a season
Set Pleasant Valley High School record for most touchdown
   passes in a game

Glossary

college recruiters: in football, people who encourage high school players to enroll at their college and play for the team

concussion: a brain injury resulting from a sharp blow to the body

contract: a deal signed by a player and a team that states the amount of money the player is paid and the number of years he or she will play

draft: a yearly event in which professional teams take turns choosing new players from a selected group

end zone: the area behind the goal line at either end of the field. To score, a team tries to get the ball into the other team's end zone.

extension: more years added to a contract to make the contract last longer

field goal: a successful kick between the U-shaped upright poles. A field goal is worth three points.

huddle: a tight circle that football players form on the field to plan the next play

intercepted: caught a pass by the opposing team's offense. When a defensive player intercepts a pass, his team gets control of the ball.

junior college: a school that offers courses similar to the first two years of college instruction

line of scrimmage: an imaginary line extending from the nose of the football to either sideline that players cannot cross until the ball is hiked

passer rating: a number, based on completions, interceptions, and other statistics, that determines a quarterback's value

playoffs: a series of games held every year to decide a league champion

polls: lists of the top teams

receiver: a player who catches passes

running back: a player whose job it is to run with the ball

scholarships: deals in which players participate in sports in exchange for money toward the cost of attending the college

spiral: a pass in which the football spins in the air. A good spiral helps a ball travel farther and with more accuracy.

tight end: a player who catches passes and blocks on rushing plays

touchdown: a six-point score. A team scores a touchdown when it gets into the other team's end zone with the ball.

wild-card game: the first round of the NFL playoffs

Further Reading & Websites

Kennedy, Mike, and Mark Stewart. *Touchdown: The Power and Precision of Football's Perfect Play*. Minneapolis: Millbrook Press, 2010.

MacRae, Sloan. *The Green Bay Packers*. New York: PowerKids Press, 2011.

Savage, Jeff. *Brett Favre*. Minneapolis: Lerner Publications Company, 2011.

Green Bay Packers: The Official Site
http://www.packers.com
The official website of the Green Bay Packers provides fans with the latest scores, team schedule, late-breaking news, biographies of Aaron Rodgers and other players, and much more.

Sports Illustrated Kids
http://www.sikids.com
The *Sports Illustrated Kids* website covers all sports, including football.

Index

Butte Community College, 14–15

Chico, California, 9
Collins, Nick, 7

Driver, Donald, 7

Favre, Brett, 20–22

Green Bay Packers, 5–8, 19, 22–26

Jennings, Greg, 7–8

Montana, Joe, 9, 17

National Football Conference (NFC) Championship, 26
National Football League (NFL), 18–19
Nelson, Jordy, 4, 6

Pittsburgh Steelers, 5, 7–8, 26
Pleasant Valley High School, 10–12

Rigsbee, Craig, 14–15

Rodgers, Aaron: attitude of, 5, 15, 17, 21, 23, 27–28; and baseball, 10, 13; birth and childhood, 9–12; college recruitment, 12–15; concussions, 25; and family, 9–10, 27; and NFL draft, 19; and Packers fans, 20, 22–23; Super Bowl MVP, 8, 26–27; and Super Bowl XLV, 4–8, 27; and teammates, 24, 27; against USC, 16–17
Rodgers, Darla (mother), 9
Rodgers, Ed (father), 9–10
Rodgers, Jordan (brother), 9
Rodgers, Luke (brother), 9–10
Roethlisberger, Ben, 7

San Francisco 49ers, 9, 19
Smith, Alex, 19
Super Bowl XLV, 4–8, 26–27

Tedford, Jeff, 15, 27

University of California–Berkeley (Cal), 15–18

Photo Acknowledgments

The images in this book are used with the permission of: AP Photo/Paul Spinelli, p. 4; © Matthew Emmons/US Presswire, pp. 5, 6; © Mark J. Rebilas/US Presswire, p. 7; AP Photo/Gary A. Vasquez, p. 8; © Anthony Dunn/Alamy, p. 9; © 2001 Photo by Bill Husa, Chico Enterprise-Record, reprinted with permission, pp. 11, 12; © 2002 Photo by Bill Husa, Chico Enterprise-Record, reprinted with permission, p. 13; © 2002 Photo by Glenn Fuentes, Chico Enterprise-Record, reprinted with permission, p. 14; AP Photo/David Zalubowski, p. 15; © Stephen Dunn/Getty Images, p. 16; © Tom Hauck/Icon SMI/ZUMA Press, p. 18; AP Photo/Julie Jacobson, p. 19; © Joe Robbins/Getty Images, p. 20; AP Photo/Donna McWilliam, p. 21; AP Photo/Morry Gash, p. 22; © Jeff Hanisch/US Presswire, p. 23; © Al Messerschmidt/Getty Images, p. 24; AP Photo/Rick Osentoski, p. 25; © Matt Freed/Pittsburgh Post-Gazette/ZUMA Press, p. 27; AP Photo/Kevin Terrell, p. 28; AP Photo/David Stluka, p. 29.

Front cover: AP Photo/Paul Jasienski.